In this comi

Beppo the Super-Monkey

Ace the Bat-Hound

Superdog

Streaky the Super-Cat

Comet the Super-Horse

Superman was sent to Earth when he was little.
Beppo went too.

Special shirt on!
SHIRTS
BLAN
SHIRTS
The rocket found Earth.
I will land here.
Whee!
Beppo landed in the jungle.

Beppo wanted to fit in.
My nose is itchy.
But instead ...
Atchoo!
Beppo wanted to help.
I'll cool you down!
Whoosh!
No! Go away, little monkey!
Beppo wanted a friend.
Nobody likes me.

Then Beppo looked up.
Maybe he will be my friend!
Superdog got a call from Ace.
A bridge is falling!
Switching to super-speed!
Beppo could see Superdog helping.
Whoosh!
I can help too.

I can fix this section.
Whoosh!
LITTER
This is my first mission!
Whoosh!
I'll check things out.

But something was wrong.
Get me down!
Oh no! What did Superdog do?
Now they will like me!

Later ...
Help! Superdog!
Steady! Keep still.
Thanks!
I need to rescue somebody too.
Gotcha!
My second mission!
Ow!
Was that Superdog?
Whoosh!

Later ...
Open up, chef!
We are hungry!
CLOSED
CLOSED
What's this?
I'll fetch some food!
Can I have some fish?
Okay, go ahead.
Thanks, Superdog!
No sweat!

Time for my third mission!
I wish I had a big fish.
Superdog!
Screech!
This fish is **too** big!

What a day!
Back to my hidden rocket!
Why are **you** here?
But I didn't do those things!
Then who did?

Bang!
Clatter!
Boom!
Now I have a rocket, too!
Abandon mission, lads!

Beppo? You are from **my** planet!
Yes, I'm Super-Monkey!
Beppo was watching me. He copied me, but he made a mess!
Whoosh!
Crash!
Sweep!
We need action!
What can we do?

Suddenly ...
I'm Comet the Super-Horse!
I'm from the future.
Wow!

The future is better, Beppo.
Will you be my friend, Comet?
Yes! Come with me!
See you in the future!
All I can say is ...

Ruff, ruff and away!